The Highlights® Big Book of Fun

Jokes, Riddles, Puzzles, and More!

Edited by Jeffrey A. O'Hare

ON THE COVER

A big sale is going on at the local super-discount store. However, the manager made a mistake and mixed up the letters on each sign. It's up to you to unscramble the words on the signs to find out what items are really on sale.

Answer on page 92

Boyds Mills Press

Published by Boyds Mills Press, Inc.
A Highlights Company
815 Church Street
Honesdale, Pennsylvania 18431
Printed in the United States of America

Publisher Cataloging-in-Publication Data

The big book of fun : jokes, riddles, puzzles, and more /
edited by Jeffrey A. O'Hare. —1st ed.
[96] p. : col. ill. ;   cm.
Summary: A collection of jokes, riddles, quizzes, and other fun
word and picture
puzzles.
ISBN 1-59078-006-X
1. Jokes — Juvenile literature. 2. Riddles — Juvenile literature.
3. Puzzles — Juvenile literature. (1. Jokes. 2. Riddles. 3. Puzzles.)
I. O'Hare, Jeffrey A. II. Title.
793.73   21   2002   CIP
2001093639

First edition, 2002
The text of this book is set in New Century Schoolbook.

Visit our Web site at www.Highlights.com

10 9 8 7 6 5 4 3 2

Ship to Shore

Sail through these adventure-filled waters to reach the island.

Illustrated by R. Michael Palan

SHADOW BOXES

Can you find the shadow of this figure?

1

2

3

4

1. Would you ever eat chopped seeds of legumes pulled from the ground mixed together with boiled fruit?

2. While on vacation, Sarah saw both the Lincoln Memorial and Monticello, which was the home of Thomas Jefferson. Yet her vacation was in Montana and she did not watch television or look in any books or magazines. How is this possible?

3. One boy behind two girls, one boy between two girls. How many children are needed to make these two statements true?

4. Blue socks and red socks are scattered in your sock drawer. If you had to get dressed in the middle of the night without any lights, what's the least number of socks you'd need to pull out of the drawer to be sure you have a pair?

Illustrated by Sherry Neidigh

Answers on page 9

SIX KNOTTY PROBLEMS

Here are six tangles of string. What happens if you pull the ends of each string? Which of them will knot, and which will come out straight?

A B C D E F

Answer on page 92

Find the Differences

Find at least seven differences in the top and bottom panels.

5

Rise and shine,

"Jimmy, it's time to get up if you want to go fishing with me."

Why are people so smart during the day?

Everything is brighter when the sun is up!

● ● ● ● ● ● ● ● ●

Which is the most optimistic food?

Toast. Even after it has been put down and has taken a lot of heat, it bounces back up.

"Sun's up!"

"Who'd like to be the first to wish me a happy birthday?"

the fun never stops.

To get the best laughs,

"Carrots?
Third aisle over."

"Porridge?
Second aisle over."

"Fabric softener?
Aisle two."

Shopper: How much are these chickens?

Grocer: Sixty cents a pound.

Shopper: Did you raise them yourself?

Grocer: Yes, sir. This morning they were only forty cents.

· ·

Mel: I'd like to buy a winter coat.

Clerk: How long would you like it?

Mel: I'll probably need it all winter.

· ·

Clerk: You should buy some spinach. It will put color in your cheeks.

Shopper: Who wants green cheeks?

you must know where to shop.

Patch Riddle

Hold the page at eye level and look across to read the riddle. Then turn the book and look across the page to read the answer.

FROM
CAKE TO BAKE

By changing only one letter at a time, you can go from CAKE to BAKE. Figure out each new word from the clues given.

C A K E

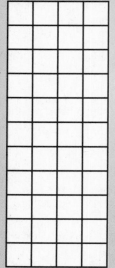

claim for yourself

gentle, no longer wild

a clock measures this

a green citrus fruit

ten cents

a round roof or ceiling

finished, completed

"acorn" of evergreen tree

a walking stick

a narrow path or road

a large body of fresh water

B A K E

Answers on page 92

Toll Trouble

Each of these cars and trucks went through the toll on the Cross Bay Bridge. Can you tell in what order they went through?

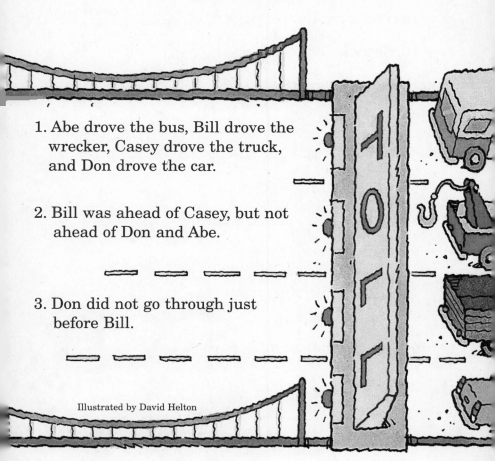

1. Abe drove the bus, Bill drove the wrecker, Casey drove the truck, and Don drove the car.

2. Bill was ahead of Casey, but not ahead of Don and Abe.

3. Don did not go through just before Bill.

Illustrated by David Helton

Ignoring the first driver over, rearrange the first letter of each remaining driver's name to find out what kind of vehicle went through fifth.

Answer on page 92

COLOR COMBOS

To solve this puzzle, write down the colorful connection between the two items given.

Quarters and Lone Ranger's horse: ☐ __ __ __ __ __

Strawberries and tomatoes: ☐ __ __

Tangerines and pumpkins: __ __ __ ☐ __ __

Mud and tree bark: __ __ __ ☐ __

Violets and lilacs: __ __ __ __ __ __

Elephants and dingy clothes: __ __ ☐ __

Night and ink: ☐ __ __ __

Sun and road signs: __ __ __ __ ☐ __

Snow and milk: __ __ ☐ __ __

Unscramble all the letters in the orange boxes to find where you might see all these colors.

__ __ __ __ __ __ __

Illustrated by Marc Nadel

ALPHABET FUN

Illustrated by Vilma Ortiz-Dillon

Answer on page 92

Find something in the picture that begins
with the letter *A*, something with *B*, *C*, and
so on for each letter of the alphabet.

K K L l M m N n O O P p Q

Riddles and Rhymes
with Our
ANIMAL FRIENDS

The answer to each riddle is two rhyming words. The clues and drawings will help you solve the riddles.

Example: What do we call a roly-poly feline?
Answer: A <u>fat</u> <u>cat</u>.

2. What sea-going vessel is commanded by Billy?

A _____ _____ .

1. What is a cotton-tailed clown?

A _____ _____ .

3. Where is an arrested aquatic mammal kept?

In a _____ _____ .

4. What is an undressed rabbit?

A _____ _____ .

5. What is a busy semiaquatic rodent when it makes baskets?

A _____ _____ .

6. What is a royal hound dog?

A _____ _____ .

7. What does a curly-tailed swine wear when it becomes bald?

A _____ _____ .

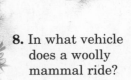

8. In what vehicle does a woolly mammal ride?

In a _____ _____ .

9. Where do two black-and-white striped mammals sleep?

In a _____ _____ .

Answer on page 92 **13**

FARM FUN

Find all these "farm" words in the letter grid. Words may appear up, down, across, backward, or diagonally. When you've found all the words, write the unused letters, from top to bottom and left to right, in the spaces below to find out who owns this farm.

The owner of this farm is

_ _ _

_ _ _ _ _ _ _ _

ANVIL
BARN
BULL
CAT
CHICKENS
CORN
COWS
CROP

DOG
DUCKS
FARMER
FENCE
FIELDS
FRUIT
GARDEN
GOATS

HAY
HOE
HOG
HORSES
HOUSE

ONION
PEN
PIGS
PLOW
PONY
ROOSTER
SHEEP
SILO

TRACTOR
TRUCK
TURKEYS
WAGON
WELL

Illustrated by Ron LeHew

```
T U R K E Y S F E N C E
O F C N E P H O U S E P
S A N V I L O O L I D O
T R A C T O R N M L C R
A M S H D W S I Y O S C
O E H I O A E O R G W D
G R E C G W S N I C O U
O O E K K A D P O W C C
H H P E C G A R D E N K
B A R N U O F I E L D S
N Y A S R N L B U L L D
F R U I T R E T S O O R
```

Answer on page 92

SILLY QUESTIONS

1. What gets beaten but never cries?
2. What can honk without a horn?
3. What has a bank but needs no money?
4. What has a ring but, alas, no finger?
5. What wears a jacket but no pants?
6. What gets a black eye without a fight?
7. What can clap without any hands?
8. What has a bark but no bite?
9. What has a horn but does not honk?

FIND THE PUPPY

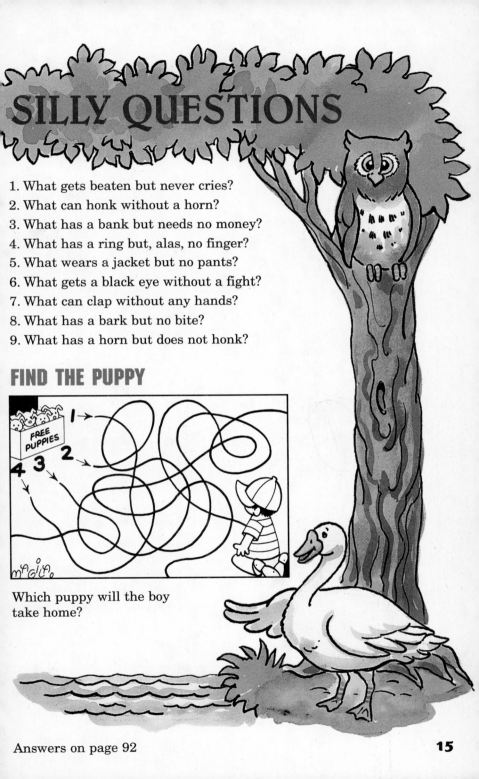

Which puppy will the boy
take home?

Boy: Dad, would you ever scold me for something I didn't do?

Father: Of course I wouldn't, son. Why do you ask?

Boy: I was just wondering because I didn't clean my room.

. . . .

Father: Before you come in the house, are your feet dirty?

Bobby: Yes, they are. But don't worry. I have my shoes on.

"Matthew said his first words today—Cluck, cluck."

"Would you rather I took my yo-yo somewhere else?"

"I said, are you warm enough?"

Father (teaching daughter to drive): Go on green, stop on red, and take it easy when I turn purple.

family life can

mothers and sons,

"Someday, son, all this will be yours."

Joel: Dad, can you write your name in the dark?

Dad: I think so.

Joel: OK, when I turn off the lights, will you sign my report card?

"Daddy, I hope you didn't try to eat the cupcake. It's plastic."

Amy: Why don't you take the bus home?

Jake: No, thanks. My parents would only make me bring it back.

Mother: Dear, would you like some more alphabet soup?

Daughter: No, thanks. I couldn't eat another syllable.

"Oh, sure, they'll come down easy. I stuck 'em up with peanut butter."

Mother: Billy, stop making faces at the bulldog.

Billy: He started it!

"Well, I think the tights go under the tutu."

e lots of fun.

Illustrated by Tim Dav

RAIN!

In this picture, can you find:

toothbrush

banana

safety pin

pencil

bell

fish

spoon

saltshaker

book

slice of pie

bird

flag

heart

horseshoe

WHO DID THAT?

Which person or creature is most likely responsible for each mishap pictured?

Answer on page 93

Illustrated by Bill Colrus

JUNK-DRAWER JUMBLE

Choose one different object from this junk drawer that could be used at each of these different events:

a wedding,
a birthday party,
an art class,
a dog show.

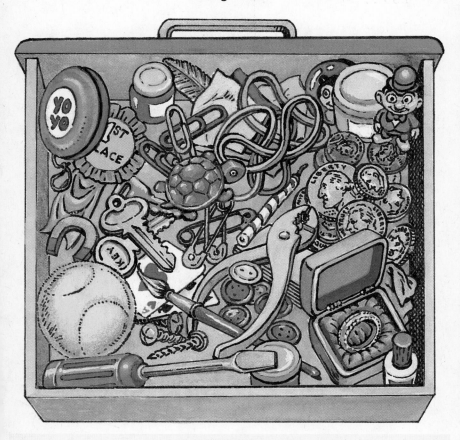

QUICK CHANGE

Dara has two coins that equal eleven cents. One of the coins is not a dime. How is this possible?

LINEUP LOGIC

The bell has sounded, and these five students have to get to class. Read the clues, and figure out the name of each student as well as what class each is trying to get to.

1. Jane is between two boys.
2. There's no one behind the student trying to get to art class.
3. The student going to music is not the first in line.
4. The boys are Morgan and Edward, one of whom is going to science.
5. The five classes are music, science, art, gym, and reading.
6. Natalie is going to reading. Jane is trying to get to gym. The other girl's name is Carol.
7. Edward had science earlier in the week, so he's going to a different class today.

Answer on page 93

Illustrated by Maggie Byer-Sprinzeles

ROAD RIDDLE

Help this lion make it across the road.
If you follow the correct route, you should go past the
letters that belong in the spaces to answer the riddle.

Why did the lion
cross the road?

Illustrated by Patti Goodnow

To get to the

~~other pride~~.

Answer on page 93

Garbage Garble

bag
are
a

Illustrated by Judith Hunt

Can you find at least
20 words using the letters
in the word

garbage?

FOUR-LEAF CLOVER

Can you find the
four-leaf clover?

answers on page 93

WANDERING WORDS

How many words of three letters or more can you find in this
"wandering" word search? Start anywhere on the grid, and move in
any direction. Do not skip over one letter to get to another. Once a
letter is used, it cannot be used again in the same word.

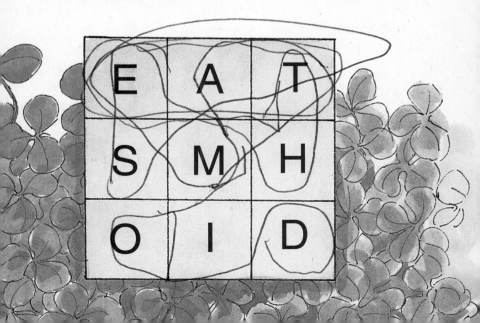

What's the hardest part of giving an elephant a bath?

Getting him into the tub.

Elephant: Doctor! Doctor! My memory is failing!

Veterinarian: When did you first notice this was happening?

Elephant: When did I first notice what was happening?

• •

Pa Snake: I hope that we're not poisonous.

Ma Snake: Why?

Pa Snake: Because I just bit my tongue.

• •

Harry Cow: How do we get rid of all this grass?

Molly Cow: Just moo it.

"I heard this zoo had some unusual animals, but I never expected this."

• • • • • • • • • • • • • • • • • • • •

What kind of cheese do dogs like on their pizza?

Mutts-arella

"I'm tired of working for peanuts."

Bird: How can we stop that rhinoceros from charging?

Turtle: Take away his credit cards.

visit a zoo

A man was sitting on the road and his truck was broken down. He had penguins in the bed of his truck. Another man stopped and asked, "Can I help?"

"Yes," said the first man. "Take these penguins to the zoo." So the second man did.

The next day the first man saw the second fellow on the street, and he still had the penguins.

The first said, "I thought I told you to take the penguins to the zoo."

The other man said, "They had so much fun at the zoo, I thought I would take them to the movies today."

● ● ● ● ● ● ● ● ● ● ● ● ● ● ● ● ● ● ●

A deer and an antelope were out playing on the prairie. The antelope suddenly stopped and cocked his head. The deer asked, "What's wrong?"

"Oh," said the antelope, "I thought I just heard a discouraging word."

What did the beaver say to the tree?

"It was nice gnawing you."

● ● ● ● ● ● ● ● ● ● ● ● ● ● ● ● ● ●

What game do rabbits play with kangaroos?

Hopscotch

● ● ● ● ● ● ● ● ● ● ● ● ● ● ● ● ● ●

What game do they both play with the toads?

Leap frog

● ● ● ● ● ● ● ● ● ● ● ● ● ● ● ● ● ●

A snail was climbing up a cherry tree when a beetle spied it. "Hey," said the beetle, "there aren't any cherries on that tree yet."

"I know," replied the snail, "but there will be by the time I get there."

"Still got that toothache?"

funnier than you.

WHAT ANIMAL IS IT?

Spell the name of an animal by using the clues given below. Write the letters in the blanks.

1. The first letter of this word is in HUG and also in HOOK.

2. The second letter is in BABY, but not in BOOK.

3. The third is in DIMPLE as well as in MAN.

4. The fourth is in SPINACH, but nowhere in CAN.

5. The fifth is in TICKLE, but never in CREAM.

6. The sixth is in FICKLE and also in DREAM.

7. The last is in RIDDLE as well as in TROT.

Now put them together and see what you've got!

__ __ __ __ __ __ __
1   2   3   4   5   6   7

Answer on page 93

28

RIDDLE CODE

Write each letter at the bottom and then read from left to right.
When you solve the code, you'll solve the riddle!
A few are done to start you off on the right note.

Riddle: Why did **The Animuscials** let the turkey
join their band?

BE

Answer on
page 93

Illustrated by Lynn Adams

Eating in or dining out

Customer: How much is coffee?

Waitress: Forty-five cents.

Customer: How much is a refill?

Waitress: It's free.

Customer: OK. I'll take a refill.

"Of course ants again!"

Customer: Waiter, is there any soup on the menu?

Waiter: No. I just wiped it off

Diner: Waitress, do you serve crabs here?

Waitress: We serve anybody! Please sit down.

"Don't put a cherry on it. Dinner's pretty soon."

Jim: I got the weather forecast from Mexico for today and tomorrow.

John: What is it?

Jim: Chili today, hot tamale.

"I don't care if it is only January. I'm hungry."

Little boy: Daddy, are bugs good to eat?

Father: Let's not talk about it at the table, son.

Father (after dinner): Now, son, what did you want to ask me?

Little boy: Oh, nothing. There was a bug in your soup, but it's gone now!

• •

Boss: Why is there a frankfurter behind your ear?

Employee: Gosh, I must have eaten my pencil for lunch!

• •

Diner: I'm in a hurry. Will my pancakes be long?

Waitress: No. Round.

• •

Customer: What is this fly doing in my soup?

Waiter: Looks like the backstroke to me.

... there's a lot to laugh about.

SHADOW BOXES

Can you find the shadow of this ship?

1

2

3

4

Illustrated by Charles Jordan

BRAIN BUSTERS

1. How many eggs can a person eat on an empty stomach?

2. In the Lang family, there are nine sisters. Each sister has one brother. How many children are in the Lang family?

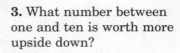

3. What number between one and ten is worth more upside down?

4. Six pine trees are in one backyard. Each pine tree has six branches. Each branch has six acorns on it. How many acorns are in the yard?

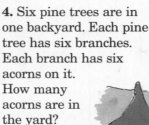

Illustrated by Maggie Byer-Sprinzeles

32

Answers on page 93

STREET SMART

Solve this crisscross puzzle by writing the given words in the correct boxes. Use the number of letters in each word to figure out where a word fits. For example, there is only one word that has nine letters. Words that share a box also share the same letter.

Alley
Avenue
Block
Boulevard
Close

Court
Drive
Highway
Lane
Parkway

Pass
Path
Place
Road
Route

Street
Terrace
Turnpike
Walk
Way

Unscramble the letters in the yellow boxes to discover one more word that belongs with the others.

CAUSEWAY

ALLEY

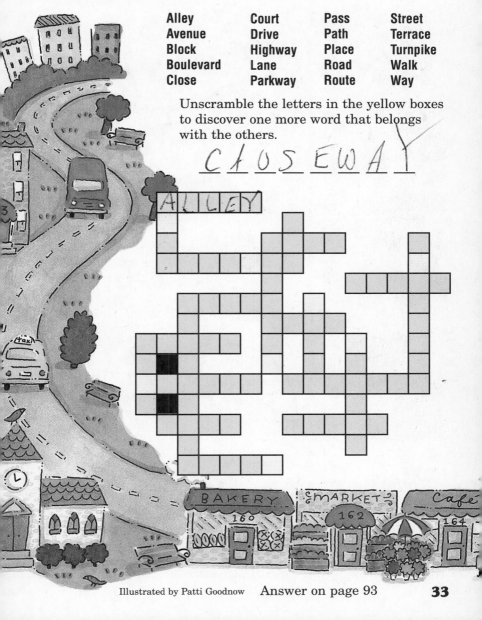

Catch the names of six fish by solving these picture puzzles.

Answer on page 93

Illustrated by David Helton

IN ITS PLACE

Each object on the left will go inside one of the objects on the right. Once you match the objects, take the first letter of each object that has a price tag. Unscramble these letters to find something that will let you see inside when you're outside, and outside when you're inside.

___ ___ ___ ___ ___ ___ ___

trated by Bill Colrus

Answer on page 93

MYSTERY PHOTOS

Identify the everyday objects in these pictures.

A

B

C

Answer on page 94

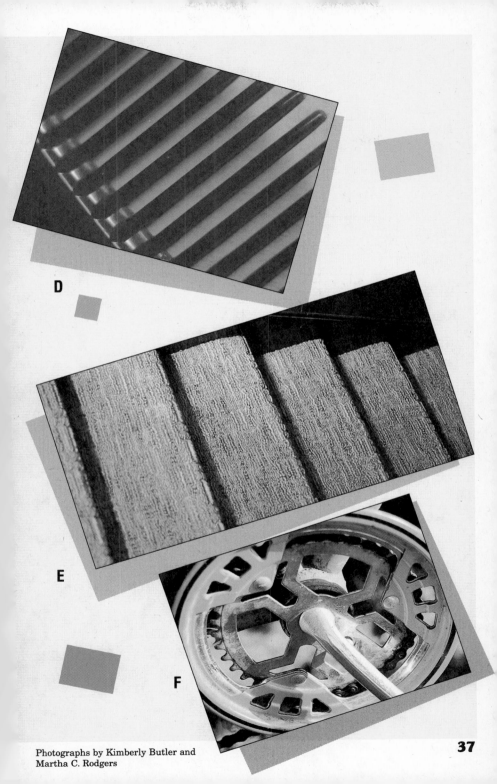

D

E

F

I WANT MY MOM

Laura, Mark, Moya, and Kevin were all born on the same day. Their moms are Sally, Judy, Meg, and Stacy. From the clues below, match each baby to his or her mother.

	Sally	Judy	Meg	Stacy
Laura				
Mark				
Moya				
Kevin				

1. Sally and Judy received blue blankets as gifts.
2. Three of the babies have the same number of letters in their names as their mothers.

LAURA   MARK   MOYA   KEVIN

Answer on page 94

HOUSEHOLD HELPERS

Unscramble the letters to spell the names of appliances and electronic equipment found around the house.

1. SLOVEINEIT _____

2. GHANIWS HEMNICA _____ _____

3. ATROSET _____

4. WORVEACIM VEON _____ _____

5. GAFIRROERRTE _____

6. ARIH DERRY _____ _____

7. PLEETHEON _____

8. MAUCUV RALNEEC _____ _____

9. RENDBEL _____

10. WISHERSHAD _____

Answer on page 94

Illustrated by Arnie Ten

Rub-a-dub-dub!

Heidi: I just got some goldfish.

Jane: Where do you keep them?

Heidi: In the bathtub.

Jane: What do you do when you take a bath?

Heidi: Blindfold them.

Who's the ringleader?

The first person in the bathtub.

"It's the only way Junior can get his dog to take a bath."

George: Why did your sister take a towel to the wedding?

Gracie: She heard the bride was having a shower.

● ●

Why did the robber take a bath?

To make a clean getaway.

● ●

What animal do you look like when you take a bath?

A little bear.

Tiny: Knock-knock!

Bubbles: Who's there?

Tiny: Dwayne.

Bubbles: Dwayne who?

Tiny: Dwayne the bathtub before it overflows!

"I stayed in twice as long, Mom. Now I don't have to do this again tomorrow."

"I guess I was a little dirty, at that."

Lots of jokes in this tub!

BUILD A BIRD

Choose one piece from
each column to build
four familiar birds.

Answer on page 94

Body Language

Change one letter in each word on the chalkboard to come up with the name of a part of your body. Then fill in the new words on the chart.

boot   bead
rose   car
top   angle
paw   chip
deck   crest

Brain Buster Bonus:

Name two other body parts that are spelled exactly the same except for one letter.

Illustrated by Ron Lieser

Answer on page 94 **43**

Number Fun

Which of these groups adds up to the highest number?

a. The number of mittens lost by the Three Little Kittens, plus the number of Snow White's dwarfs, plus the number of ghosts that visit Ebenezer Scrooge.

b. The number of corners on King Arthur's Round Table, plus the number of blackbirds baked in a pie, plus the number of Things in the hat of the Cat in the Hat.

c. The number of bags of wool from "Baa, Baa, Black Sheep," plus the number of fiddlers called by Old King Cole, plus the number of blue oxen owned by Paul Bunyan.

BONUS: Add all three totals together to find the number of states in the United States.

SHADOW BOXES

Find the silhouette for this scene.

1

2

3

4

Illustrated by Charles Jordan

WHAT'S WRONG?

Can you spot what's unusual in each scene?

1.

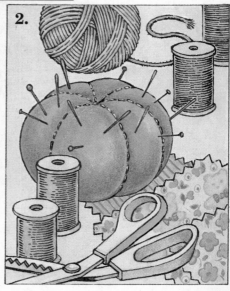

2.

3.

4.

Illustrated by Marc Nadel

Answer on page 94

Illustrated by Charles Jorda

RABBIT AND TURTLE RACE

In this picture, can you find:

slice of
cake

feather

pencil

nail

crescent
moon

musical note

spoon

pushpin

ice-cream
cone

safety pin

carrot

slice of pie

magic wand

ROAMING NUMERALS

12	3	5	17	19	4	1
9	10	11	23	16	14	15
8	7	5	90	13	27	6
33	34	35	2	39	44	55
78	79	87	67	73	61	26
41	40	45	46	48	47	78
19	3	18	21	83	96	99

Connect all the even numbers shown to reach the middle. Start at
the 12 in the top row, and end at the 2 in the center. You can move
across, down, or diagonally, but your line may not cross itself.

Illustrated by David Helton

ALL IN
BLACK AND WHITE

These coded words name things that are black and white. Each letter stands for another letter. The code is the same throughout this puzzle. For example, Q stands for the letter O. All other Qs in this puzzle also stand for the letter O. If you think about the relationship between Q and O, you'll have a good clue to help decode this list.

1.
eqqmkgu

2.
urggf-nkokv ukip

3.
pgyurcrgt

4.
fkeg

5.
umwpm

6.
qnf rjqvqitcrj

7.
ejguu rkgegu

8.
fcnocvkcp

9.
bgdtc

10.
rkcpq mgau

The doctor is here

Patient: Doctor, I'm not well. I keep thinking I'm a Great Dane.

Doctor: How long have you been feeling this way?

Patient: Ever since I was a puppy.

· ·

Doctor: Your cough sounds much better today.

Patient: It should. I've been practicing all night!

· ·

Doctor: You'll have to stop thinking about your problems so much. Throw yourself into your work!

Patient: But, Doctor, I mix cement!

· ·

Milkman: Are you sure you want fifty-four quarts of milk?

Lady: Yes, my doctor told me to take a bath in milk.

Milkman: Do you want it pasteurized?

Lady: No, just up to my chin.

What do you give a sick bird?

Tweetment

· ·

Where do wasps go if they get hurt?

The waspital

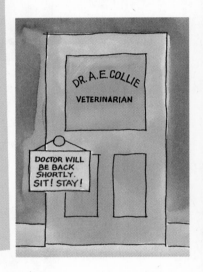

"You've got to cut out the 'between-meal' snacks."

DEAR DR. RIDDLE:

"Hello, Doctor! I'm the bug that's been going around."

What happens when the human body is completely surrounded by water?
>Signed,
>Soaking Sam

Dear Sam:
The phone rings.
>Dr. R.

••••••••••••••••••••••••••••••••••••

Dear Dr. Riddle:
How do you make antifreeze?
>Yours truly,
>Polar Paul

Dear Polar:
Put ice cubes in her sleeping bag.
>Dr. R.

••••••••••••••••••••••••••••••••••••

Dear Dr. Riddle:
How can I cure myself of sleepwalking?
>The Wanderer

Dear Wanderer:
Sprinkle thumbtacks on your bedroom floor.
>Dr. R.

••••••••••••••••••••••••••••••••••••

Dear Dr. Riddle:
I have this problem. Half the time I think I'm a wigwam, and the other half I think I'm a teepee.
>Signed,
>Who Am I?

Dear Who:
Sit down and relax. You're two tents (too tense).
>Dr. R.

with a dose of good cheer!

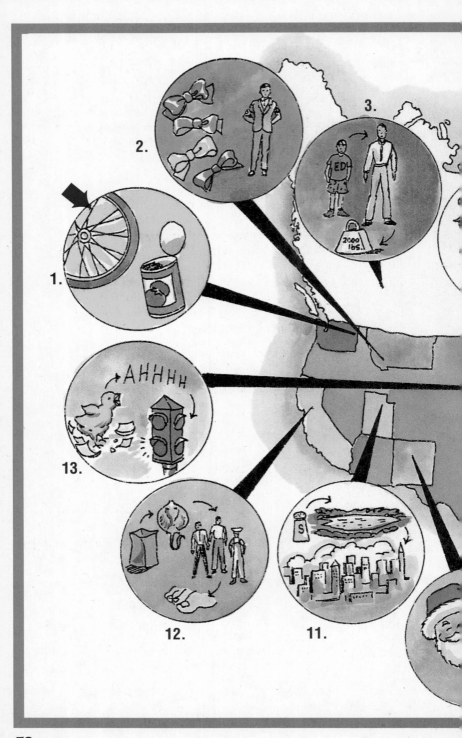

Name That City

Can you guess these North American cities from the clues below?

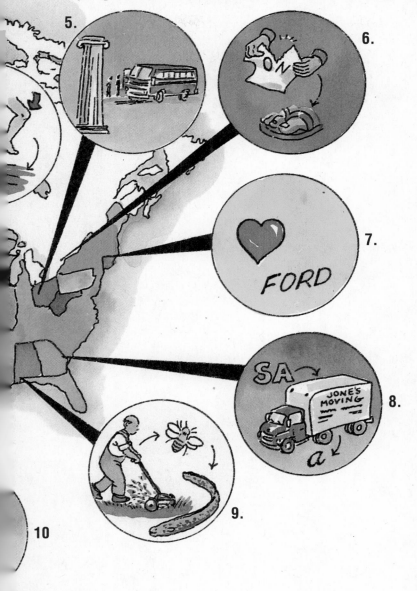

5.

6.

7.

8.

9.

10

Crossword Riddle

Read each clue, then write the answers in the appropriate boxes. When you've filled in the grid, put the letters from eight numbered boxes in the matching boxes on the treasure chest to spell out the answer to the riddle.

ACROSS

1. Move about in the water
5. Toys that fly and have tails
7. You may get this color from the sun.
8. Short sleep
10. Painting or sculpture
11. Negative answer
12. Summertime pests
14. Not even
15. Not fresh
17. Actors perform in these.
19. Belonging to us
20. Not as moist as some
22. Abbreviation for *Utah*

23. Unwelcome picnic guest
24. Need this to fish
26. Belonging to that boy
27. Past tense of *rise*, the dough has _____.
29. Small boat

Mystery Riddle:
What kind of coffee do fish drink?

12	3	8	15	7	23	11	16

DOWN

1. Glide on rollers or blades
2. Come in first
3. That thing
4. Grown-up boys
6. What the beach is, or Orphan Annie's dog
7. Attempted
9. What peas grow in
10. Everybody together
12. Distant
13. What a top does
14. Use this to row

15. How a lemon tastes
16. One-on-one teacher
18. Allow
21. Wet weather
25. Past tense of *do*
26. That girl
28. Do, re, mi, fa, __

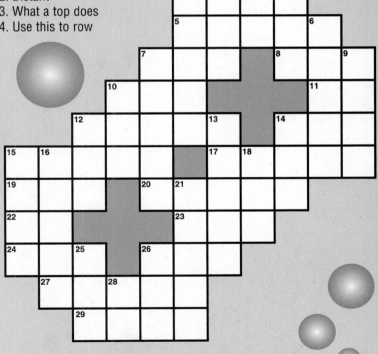

Illustrated by Karen Stormer Brooks

Answer on page 94

Why do baseball games have to be played at night?

Because the bats sleep in the daytime.

• •

Why does it take longer to get from second base to third base than it does to get to second from first?

Because there's a shortstop in between second and third.

• •

If athletes have athlete's foot, then what do astronauts have?

Missile-toe

"I think he's going to slide into home."

"We called the game on account of mud."

"You can play with it. But don't kick it or drop it in the dirt. It's brand new."

Soccer player: Say, why didn't you stop the ball?

New Goalie: I thought that's what the net was for!

. . . .

A dog catcher

Why does it get so hot after a basketball game?

Because all the fans are gone.

. . . .

Jan left home, made three left turns, and when she got home again, there were two masked people waiting for her. Who were they?

The catcher and the umpire.

. . . .

How could a baseball team win 7-0 if not one single person touched home plate?

All the players who scored runs were married.

. . . .

If the Navy and Marines were playing basketball and all of the Marines fouled out, who would the team send in next?

Submarines

look at sports and have a ball!

Fitness Fun

Let's keep fit by eating right, exercising, and fitting the following words into their correct spaces in this puzzle. Use the size of each word as a clue to where it fits. Only one letter goes in each box.

Yoga
Dance
Karate
Soccer
Tennis
Fencing
Jogging
Running
Skating

Aerobics
Exercise
Swimming
Nutrition
Basketball
Gymnastics
Volleyball
Racquetball
Weight lifting

Illustrated by Lynn Adams

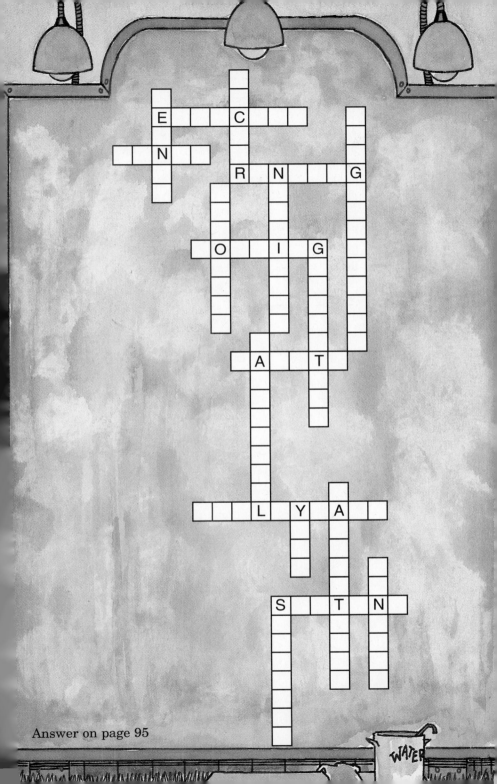

Answer on page 95

SILLY SOUNDS

Circle these sounds in the word search below. Search forward, backward, up, down, or diagonally to find each word.

BANG
BUZZ
CHIME
CLAP
CLICK
CRACKLE
CRASH
CREAK
DRIP

GURGLE
HISS
HUM
KNOCK
PING
POP
RATTLE
RING
RUMBLE

SNAP
SQUEAK
SQUEAL
SWISH
TAP
THUMP
TICK
WHAM
WHISTLE

```
Z L P I N G E L K C A R C
T Z C R E P O P O M B L E
I G U R R I N G C R A S H
C R A B G U G T I P P I U
K N O C K S U R A T T L E
H U A E S P R A E P I N M
G I N I A O G S W I S H I
T S H N S T L E B A N G H
W H S A C R E A K P A C C
S Q U E A L E L T S I H W
K N O M S Q U E A K H I H
R A T T P P I R D A B U A
E L B M U R H C L I C K M
```

Answer on page 95   Illustrated by Anni Matsick

OBSERVE IT

Chef Leroy is having a bad day. Study this picture for thirty seconds. Then try to answer all the questions on the next page without looking back at the picture again.

Illustrated by Lynn Adams

"OBSERVE IT" QUESTIONS

Stop! Don't read these until you've looked at the picture on page 61.

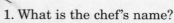

1. What is the chef's name?
2. Is the chef wearing a hat?
3. Is there a dog or a cat in the picture?
4. Is the chef wearing an apron?
5. Is there milk on the table?
6. How many eggs did you see?
7. What spilled on the table?
8. How many lamps are in the picture?
9. Does the chef wear eyeglasses?
10. Is there a spider in the picture?
11. Which shaker has a letter on it, the salt or the pepper?
12. What object is flying through the air?

DOZEN DONUTS

Using the numbers 1, 2, 3, 4, 5, 6, and 7 only once, fill these donuts so that each row across, down, and diagonally adds up to 12.

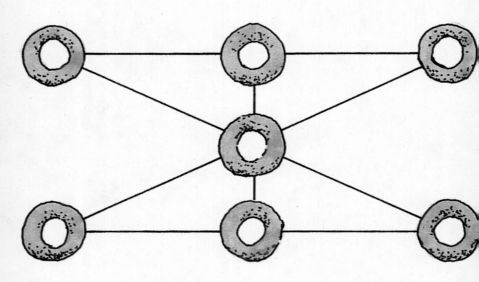

SHOE BUSINESS

These customers are waiting to get their footwear fixed at Frantic Frank's Fantastic Footwear Factory. Match each customer to the boots or shoes he or she needs.

After you've matched the footwear to the owner, look at the letter on the tag of each pair. Start with the pair that belongs to the first customer in line, and put the letters in order on the lines below. You'll find out whether Frank was able to fix all the footwear.

He was not

_ _ _ _ _ _ _ .

SHADOW BOXES

Can you find the shadows of these giraffes?

Illustrated by Charles Jordan

BRAIN BUSTERS

1. A rooster is sitting on top of a barn. The roof slopes down to the left and to the right. A wind is blowing to the right at fifteen miles per hour. If the rooster lays an egg atop the barn, which way will the egg roll, to the right or to the left?

2. Farmer Brown combined two piles of hay from one field with three piles of hay from another field. How many piles does he now have?

3. You're driving a bus. At the first stop, three people get on. At the next stop, one person gets off, and two others get on. At the third stop, four people get off and one young lady gets on. At the fourth stop, five people get on and two get off.

a. How many people are now on the bus?

b. What is the bus driver's name?

Illustrated by David Helton

MAGIC SQUARES

These eight words can fit into the magic square below. The words will read either across or down, and only one letter will go into each box. It's up to you to figure out how to fit in all eight words.

COME   KNEE   OVEN
CORK   MADE   REDS
ELSE   OVAL

Place the numbers 1 through 9 in the squares of this grid so that the total of any three boxes, across, down, or diagonally, will equal 15.

Illustrated by Beth Griffis Johnson

Answer on page 95

COUNT ON IT

Try these challenging number puzzles on your friends.

1. Ask someone to think of any whole number higher than 1. Then ask him to
- multiply the number by 6,
- divide it by 3,
- multiply the new total by 2,
- divide by 4,
- add 10 to the new total,
- subtract the number he thought of, and
- divide the remainder by 5.

Now you can reveal the answer. It will always be the same, no matter what number you start with.

2. You can convince anyone that you have eleven fingers. Hold out both hands and start counting down: 10, 9, 8, etc. Put one finger down on the same hand with each count until you reach the number 6, which should complete one hand. Now say, "That's six, plus five fingers on my other hand equals eleven."

3. You can guess a person's secret number. Ask her to think of any whole number of 1 or higher. Then ask her to
- multiply the number by 3,
- add 1 to the new number,
- multiply the new number by 3, and
- add her original number to this new total.

Now ask for her current number. Pretend to go into a deep trance as you try to mentally grab her original number from the air.

The trick: Just remove the number in the "ones" place (the last numeral) from her current total. The remaining number or numbers will be the original number she chose.

Mystery Guest

Read each clue. Fill in the answers to each statement in the spaces provided. Then write the numbered letters in the corresponding boxes at the bottom of the puzzle to find the name of our mystery guest.

1. Longest river in the United States:

___ ___ ___ ___ ___ ___ ___ ___
 3   4

2. Flat floating object: ___ ___ ___ ___
                         9   1

3. Name of a dark blue fruit:

___ ___ ___ ___ ___ ___ ___ ___ ___
                          8   7

4. Without shoes: ___ ___ ___ ___ ___ ___ ___ ___
                                      2

5. Pen name of Samuel Clemens:

___ ___ ___ ___ ___ ___ ___ ___ ___
   5   6

☐ ☐ ☐   ☐ ☐ ☐ ☐ ☐ ☐
1 2 3   4 5 6 7 8 9

Illustrated by Marc Nadel

Answer on page 95

YOUR NOSE KNOWS

Sniff out all these smells in the word search by looking up, down, forward, backward, and diagonally. The leftover letters, when read left to right and top to bottom, will spell one of the most delicious smells of all.

ammonia	fish	onion	soap
apple	gasoline	orange	strawberry
banana	grass	peach	thyme
bread	ham	peanut butter	turkey
broccoli	hamburger	pepper	vanilla
cabbage	hay	pizza	vinegar
cake	leather	rain	wet dog
chocolate	lemon	rose	
cinnamon	lily	sage	
clove	mint	skunk	

```
G R A S S T R A W B E R R Y
P C I N N A M O N I O N H C
E E V C A B B A G E O M A H
P H A M B U R G E R T B U O
P S N N T T E A N A N A B C
E I I P U S A G E G N A R O
R F L E R T D S K E T L O L
E Y L A K R B K A N T E C A
W Y A C E P P U C I H A C T
E P O H Y A L N T V Y T O E
T I C L O V E K P T M H L M
D Z C S O R M R O S E E I I
O Z N A M M O N I A R R L N
G A S O L I N E L P P A Y T
```

Illustrated by Anni Matsick

Laughter is easy to find,

A frog went into the bank to get a loan. He went to a bank teller named Patty Black and said, "May I have a loan?"

She asked the frog if he had any collateral so that she could approve the loan. The frog replied that he had only a little statue.

Patty Black took the statue to the bank manager and asked if it was OK to give the frog the money.

The manager looked at the statue and said, "It's a knick-knack, Patty Black. Give the frog a loan!"

"I stayed home and had roast beef. He went to market and I haven't seen him since."

"OK, kids, here's our summer cottage."

"Which one of you is the candlestick maker?"

70

"Don't tell me. I know. You've been following Mary again!"

"Now be careful! A pail of water isn't worth a broken crown."

What did the Cinderella fish wear to the ball?

Glass flippers

• •

Why did Humpty Dumpty have a great fall?

To make up for having a bad summer.

• •

Who wrote the book *Baker's Men?*

Pat E. Cake

• •

What do you get when you cross a book of nursery rhymes and an orange?

Mother Juice

even in nursery rhymes.

Butcher: The candlestick maker's job keeps him pretty busy every Saturday and Sunday.

Baker: Doesn't he work during the week?

Butcher: No, just on wick ends.

• •

Ladybug: Hello, fire department? Come quickly, my house is on fire!

Chief: How do we get there?

Ladybug: Don't you still have your big red truck?

• •

Snow White: Why was Cinderella standing outside the photography shop?

Rose Red: She was waiting for her prints to come.

• •

Mother Goose: Can you name twelve animals that appear in nursery rhymes?

Lucy Locket: Three bears, three little kittens, three blind mice, and three little pigs.

• •

Boy Blue: I played "The Star-Spangled Banner" for hours and hours.

Tommy Tucker: So what? I can sing "The Stars and Stripes Forever."

• •

Jack: What happened when one of the King's men told Humpty Dumpty a joke?

Jill: I don't know.

Jack: He fell for it.

"The King is in his counting house."

"Where are the three little pigs?"

"That's easy for you to say!"

"Not only has someone been sleeping in our beds . . . All the TVs are turned to the EDUCATIONAL station!"

"This microwave has only three settings. Too hot, too cold, and just right."

"She's about 5 feet 7 inches, black hair, flawless complexion . . ."

Old Mother Hubbard went to the cupboard to get her poor dog a bone. But when she got there, the cupboard was bare, so the dog took off to live with the Spratt family.

"Oh, dear! I've forgotten if the recipe calls for four or twenty."

DELIVERY DAZE

Find the path that leads to the supermarket loading dock. You can't cross over or go back along your path at any time. As you drive along, pick up the letters you pass to find the cargo you're delivering to the grocery store.

— — — — — — — —

Answer on page 96

MYSTERY CROSSWORD

Unscramble each clue. Then write the correct word in the boxes. Study the clues to see if you can identify the mystery person that has all these things in common. You can check your answer against the circled letters in the grid. Of course, you'll have to unscramble them, too.

ACROSS
3. RPOO
4. AMN
7. NILISOIL
8. LATL
10. RAW
11. TUNYKKEC
12. DIRSPEENT

DOWN
1. ONHSET
2. BACIN
5. VALERYS
6. SONGCRES
9. RAYLEW

The mystery person is

___ ___ ___ ___ ___ ___ ___ .

Illustrated by Vilma Ortiz-Dillon

Answer on page 96

Even at school, fun can be the rule.

What do you call a duck that gets all A's?

A wise quacker

Where was the Declaration of Independence signed?

At the bottom.

What did the math book say to the calculator?

"I really have a lot of problems, so I'm counting on you."

Who invented the first airplane that didn't fly?

The Wrong brothers

Father: Well, son, how are your grades this marking period?

Son: Underwater.

Father: What do you mean by that?

Son: They're below "C" level.

• •

Cassandra: How do you spell *Mississippi?*

Sally: Which one, the river or the state?

• •

Teacher: Mary, tell me what they did at the Boston Tea Party.

Mary: I don't know. I wasn't invited.

• •

Teacher: Freddy, give me a sentence using the word *fascinate.*

Freddy: I have nine buttons on my jacket, but I can only fasten eight.

"This wasn't so bad. I may be back tomorrow."

"It was nice of your father, but we prefer that students use desks provided by the school."

Why can't you play hide-and-seek with a mountain?

Because the mountain peaks.

"Hurry up and teach your brother how to count to a hundred so we can play hide-and-seek."

"How did you make out at the kite-flying contest?"

Dad: Why didn't you play school with your sister?

Junior: I did. I played I was absent.

• •

Bert: Mom, can I go out and play?

Mom: What? With those torn trousers?

Bert: No, with the kid across the street.

• •

Minnie: Did you hear about the new doctor doll?

Winnie: No.

Minnie: Just wind him up and he operates on batteries.

• •

Clerk: Now this model walks, talks, cries, and drinks water.

Little girl: I have a baby sister who does that. I just want a doll.

GAME CROSSING

And at the end of the day, there's still time for play.

Illustrated by R. Michael Pala

DOGS IN THE POOL

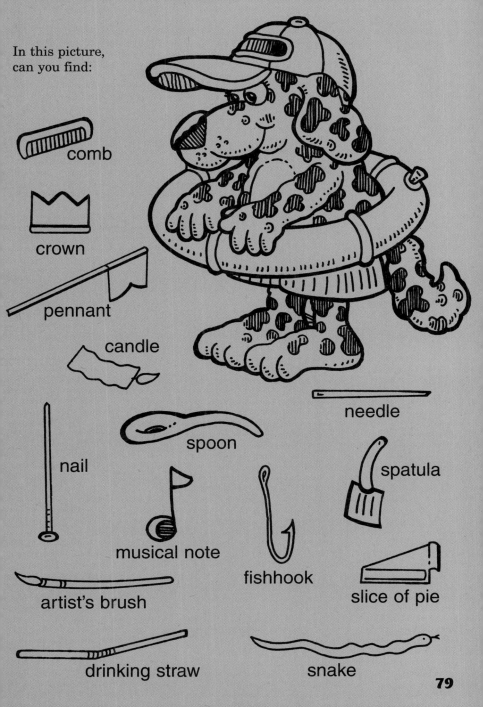

In this picture,
can you find:

comb

crown

pennant

candle

needle

nail

spoon

spatula

musical note

fishhook

slice of pie

artist's brush

drinking straw

snake

What's the Forecast?

Unscramble the weather words. Then place the numbered letters on the numbered blanks at the bottom to find the forecast.

1. wons __ __ __ __
                  4

2. steel __ __ __ __ __
                9 5 3

3. lhai __ __ __ __
        8 6

4. dwni __ __ __ __
        1

5. ianr __ __ __ __
       10

6. stim __ __ __ __
                 7

7. hundret __ __ __ __ __ __ __
                              2

Forecast:

__ __ __ __ __ __ __ __ __ __
 1 2 3   4 5 6 7 8 9 10

Illustrated by Ron Lieser   Answer on page 96

PRETTY POLLY

Answer each statement with a word made
from the letters in PARROT.

1. What you use to row a boat: _____

2. Something to cook in: _____

3. Decay: _____

4. Black, gooey road covering: _____

5. Rodent: _____

6. Opposite of bottom: _____

7. A small measure of butter: _____

8. Strike hard, as on a door: _____

9. Strike gently, as with a finger: _____

10. Statues and paintings: _____

11. Sound of a lion: _____

12. Place where a ship comes in: _____

Illustrated by Marc Nadel

BONUS PUZZLE: Add the word IT to the letters in PARROT to
get a new word that means "picture." Hint: You will need to
switch the letters into new positions.

Answer on page 96

SHADOW BOXES

Can you find the shadow of this windmill and waterwheel?

1

2

3

4

BRAIN BUSTERS

1. Can a person see farther at night or during the day?

2. Without taking time to count, can you identify the fifth letter of the alphabet? How about the tenth? Now try for the twentieth.

Q A I P C H
F L T M K Z
G E R N U D
V O X J Y B S W

3. Here's good news about your allowance. You can either have a dollar a day for thirty-one days, or you can start with a penny and double your total every day for each of those thirty-one days. (On the first day you get one penny. On the second day you get two pennies. On the third you get four pennies. On the fourth you get eight pennies, and so on.) Which option would you choose?

4. How much would you pay for seventeen roses if they were marked $12 for a dozen?

Answers on page 96

Instru-Mental

Use your brain power to identify the instruments described. Write the letters for each answer in the spaces provided. Once you list all the correct instruments, read down the blue column to find a bonus word that is related to music.

1. A stringed instrument made by Stradivarius: _ _ ▪ _ _ _

2. Keyboard instrument whose name sounds like a part of the body: _ ▪ _ _ _

3. Metal disks that crash when played: ▪ _ _ _ _ _ _ _

4. Alto or tenor wind instruments. Some look like the letter J.: _ _ _ _ _ _ ▪ _ _ _ _

5. A large member of the violin family: _ ▪ _ _ _

6. Largest instrument of violin family: _ _ ▪ _

7. Largest brass instrument: ▪ _ _ _

8. Timpani and chimes are in this family of instruments: _ _ ▪ _ _ _ _ _ _ _

9. Keyboard instrument whose name means "soft" in Italian: _ _ _ ▪ _ _

Illustrated by Charles Micucci

Bonus word: _ _ _ _ _ _ _ _ _ _

Answer on page 96

MOM!

Can you tell which offspring came
from which egg?

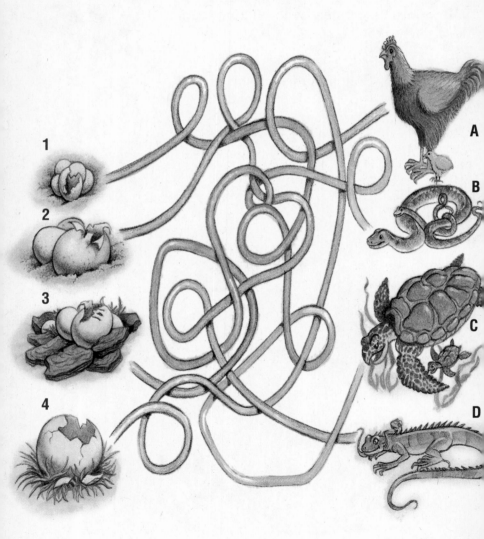

Illustrated by Franklin Ay

COMMON BONDS

Look at the objects in each vertical column. What do they have in common?

Illustrated by Brad Marks

Answer on page 96

Letter Perfect

In the rows below, one letter can be added before each word to form all new words. The letter will be the same for all the words in the same row. Once you've discovered all the missing letters, write them in order in the spaces below to find a reward.

1. ___ill   ___own   ___rant   ___rate
2. ___we   ___pen   ___men   ___ink
3. ___edge   ___eave   ___east   ___ion
4. ___rill   ___art   ___are   ___ark
5. ___tack   ___eat   ___hoe   ___urge
6. ___in   ___one   ___win   ___rack
7. ___cross   ___round   ___bout   ___corn
8. ___at   ___ace   ___am   ___eel

You get a ___ ___ ___ ___ ___ ___ ___ .

Illustrated by Ron Lieser

Answer on page 96

PICTURE PUZZLES

Look at the picture clues to figure out what common word or phrase is being shown. (If you're stumped, try unscrambling the letters under the pictures.)

1. sraque naced

2. erbad xob

3. tho odg

4. lamp tere

5. slipelgn ebe

6. lejlyshif

7. mtoaot alptn

8. hocols fo sihf

9. yfl lalb

Answer on page 96

SECRET OF THE RINGS

Walk-in-the-Water was the name of something famous in history. You can find out what it was by solving the letter-ring puzzle below. Going from left to right, look carefully at the letters inside the rings. In the blanks below, copy down in order only the letters you find inside the unlinked rings. The letters will spell out the answer.

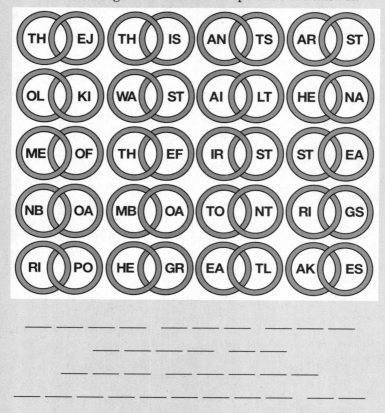

—— —— —— —— —— —— ——

—— —— —— —— —— ——

—— —— —— —— —— —— ——

—— —— —— —— —— —— —— ——

—— —— —— —— —— ——

—— —— —— —— .

Answer on page 96

PRESIDENTS' MONEY MATCH

Match each bill or coin to the U.S. President who appears on it.
Two Presidents are used twice. One has been done for you.

1. $1 ___   **A. Abraham Lincoln**

2. penny ___   **B. George Washington**

3. quarter ___   **C. Thomas Jefferson**

4. nickel ___   **D. Andrew Jackson**

5. $5 ___   **E. Grover Cleveland**

6. $500 ___   **F. William McKinley**

7. dime ___   **G. Franklin D. Roosevelt**

8. $1,000 _E_   **H. John F. Kennedy**

9. half-dollar ___

10. $20 ___   Answer on page 96

"Do you have any
'get welded soon' cards?"

JOKES

Corky: How do you keep a friend in suspense?

Karen: I don't know. How?

Corky: I'll tell you later.

• •

Teacher: Before we start working on our class play, tell me, who has had any stage experience?

Student: My leg was in a cast once.

Get ready for a load

Barney: I've owned this car for fifteen years and never had a wreck.

Prospective buyer: You mean you have had this wreck for fifteen years and never had a car!

• • • • • • • • • • • • • • • •

Joe: Did you hear about the man who dreamed he was a muffler?

Mae: No.

Joe: He woke up exhausted.

• • • • • • • • • • • • • • • •

Small-Car Owner: I'll take a quart of gasoline and two ounces of oil.

Gas Station Attendant: OK. Would you like me to sneeze in your tires, too?

"That's it!"

What goes down a hill but never moves?

A road

• •

If all the cars in the country were pink, what would we have?

A pink carnation

of laughs on the road.

Answers

SHOPPING SCRAMBLE (cover)
POTS-TOPS   HOSES-SHOES
LUMPS-PLUMS   PETALS-PLATES
CHARTS-STARCH   TAPES-PASTE
PAGERS-GRAPES   OCEANS-CANOES
AUNT-TUNA

SHIP TO SHORE
(page 3)

SHADOW BOXES (page 4)
Number 1

BRAIN BUSTERS (page 4)
1. That's a fancy way of saying "peanut butter and jelly."
2. Sarah looked at the coins in her pocket. The Lincoln Memorial is on the back of a penny, and Monticello is on the back of a nickel.
3. Four (girl, girl, boy, girl).
4. Three. Even if you pick a blue and a red sock, your third selection will match one of these colors.

SIX KNOTTY PROBLEMS (page 5)
Only A, C, and F will knot.

PATCH RIDDLE (page 8)
1. When is a new umberella old?
2. When it is used up.

FROM CAKE to BAKE (page 8)
CAKE, take, tame, time, lime, dime, dome, done, cone, cane, lane, lake, BAKE

TOLL TROUBLE (page 9)
The drivers went through in this order: Don, Abe, Bill, and Casey.

If you rearrange the initials of Abe, Bill, and Casey, you'll know that the fifth vehicle to go through the toll was a CAB.

COLOR COMBOS (page 10)
S ilver   bro W n   B lack
R ed   purple   yell O w
ora N ge   gr A y   wh I te

Where might you see these : RAINBOWS

ALPHABET FUN (page 11)
We found Apple, Banana, Cup, Dog, Egg, Fringe, Grapes, Horse, Icicles, Jam, Keys, Lamp, Mouse, Needles, Orange, Pear, Quilt, Rug, Snow, Table, Umbrella, Vase, Window, Xylophone, Yarn, Zipper. You may have found other answers.

RIDDLES AND RHYMES WITH OUR
ANIMAL FRIENDS (pages 12-13)
1. funny bunny   6. regal beagle
2. goat boat   7. pig wig
3. whale jail   8. sheep jeep
4. bare hare   9. skunk bunk
5. beaver weaver

FARM FUN (page 14)

The owner is OLD MACDONALD.

SILLY QUESTIONS (page 15)
1. An egg   6. A black-eyed pea
2. A goose   7. Thunder
3. A river   8. A tree
4. A telephone   9. A rhinoceros
5. A book

FIND THE PUPPY (page 15)
Puppy 3

WHO DID THAT? (page 20)
1-B, 2-H, 3-C, 4-F, 5-D, 6-A, 7-I, 8-G, 9-E

JUNK-DRAWER JUMBLE (page 21)
Wedding-Ring, Birthday-Candle,
Art class-Paintbrush, Dog show-Blue ribbon

QUICK CHANGE (page 21)
One of Dara's coins is a penny. It's her
other coin that is a dime.

LINEUP LOGIC (page 22)
Jane is fourth (clue 1). She's going to gym
(clue 6). Either Morgan or Edward is last
(clue 4). Since Edward is not going to science
(clue 7), he is going to art (clue 2). That
means Edward is last. So Morgan is third,
and he's going to science. The music student
is not first (clue 3), so she is second. That
only leaves the first spot for the reading
student. So Natalie is first (clue 6), and
Carol is second.

So the answer is as follows:
First - Natalie - reading class,
Second - Carol - music class,
Third - Morgan - science class,
Fourth - Jane - gym class,
Fifth - Edward - art class.

ROAD RIDDLE (page 23)
Why did the lion cross the road?
To get to the OTHER PRIDE.

GARBAGE GARBLE (page 24)
Here are our words. You may find others.
age, are, area, baa, bag, bar, bare, barge,
bear, beg, berg, brag, ear, egg, era, gab, gag,
gage, gar, garage, garb, grab, rag, rage.

FOUR-LEAF CLOVER (page 25)

WANDERING WORDS (page 25)
Here are some words we found. You may
have found others.

AMID	HAS	MATH	SEAM
DIM	HAT	MEAT	SEAT
DIME	HID	MESA	SEMI
DIMES	HIM	SAME	SOME
EAT	HIS	SAT	TAME
HAM	MAT	SEA	THIS

WHAT ANIMAL IS IT? (page 28)
1. H 2. A 3. M 4. S 5. T 6. E 7. R
The animal is "HAMSTER."

RIDDLE CODE (page 29)
Because he had his own drumsticks.

SHADOW BOXES (page 32)
Number 1

BRAIN BUSTERS (page 32)
1. One. After that, the stomach isn't empty.
2. Ten. Nine girls and one boy.
3. The number 6. Turn it upside down,
   and it becomes the number 9.
4. None. Pine trees don't have acorns.
   They have pine cones.

STREET SMART (page 33)

Bonus word: CAUSEWAY

LOOKS FISHY TO ME (page 34)
1. Perch 2. Carp 3. Herring 4. Tuna
5. Rainbow trout 6. Catfish

IN ITS PLACE (page 35)
Pearl in oyster shell; violin in violin
case; flower in flowerpot; tape in tape
dispenser; film in camera; crayons in
crayon box; picture in frame; bucket in
well; quill in inkwell; fish in net; socks in
drawer; turkey in oven; photographs in
wallet; shoelace in shoe.

Mystery word: WINDOWS

MYSTERY PHOTOS (pages 36-37)

A. reinforcements   D. comb
B. pencils   E. stairway
C. looseleaf binder   F. bicycle sprocket

I WANT MY MOM (page 38)

Laura's mom is Stacy, Mark's mom is Judy, Moya's mom is Meg, Kevin's mom is Sally.

HOUSEHOLD HELPERS (page 39)

1. TELEVISION   2. WASHING MACHINE
3. TOASTER   4. MICROWAVE OVEN
5. REFRIGERATOR   6. HAIR DRYER
7. TELEPHONE   8. VACUUM CLEANER
9. BLENDER   10. DISHWASHER

BUILD A BIRD (page 42)

A-H-J = Pelican   B-G-I = Ostrich
C-E-L = Eagle   D-F-K = Penguin

BODY LANGUAGE (page 43)

boot-foot   bead-head
rose-nose   car-ear
top-toe   angle-ankle
paw-jaw   chip-chin
deck-neck   crest-chest

BRAIN BUSTER: waist and wrist or hip and lip.

NUMBER FUN (page 44)

a. $6 + 7 + 4 = 17$
b. $0 + 24 + 2 = 26$
c. $3 + 3 + 1 = 7$

All three totals together equal 50 states in the Union.

SHADOW BOXES (page 44)

Number 4

WHAT'S WRONG? (page 45)

1. You would not be able to see a star in the crescent.
2. The needles have no eyes.
3. Robins are born without feathers.
4. Even-numbered pages are always on the left-hand side of a book, odd on the right-hand side.

ROAMING NUMERALS (page 48)

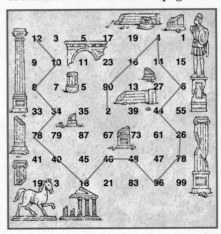

ALL IN BLACK AND WHITE (page 49)

1. cookies   6. old photograph
2. speed-limit sign   7. chess pieces
3. newspaper   8. dalmatian
4. dice   9. zebra
5. skunk   10. piano keys

NAME THAT CITY (pages 52-53)

1. Spokane   5. Columbus   10. Santa Fe
2. Bozeman   6. Toronto   11. Salt Lake City
3. Edmonton   7. Hartford   12. Sacramento
4. Winnipeg   8. Savannah   13. Chicago
          9. Mobile

CROSSWORD RIDDLE (pages 54-55)

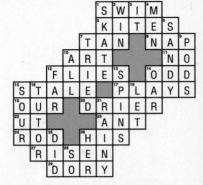

What kind of coffee do fish drink?
FINSTANT

FITNESS FUN (pages 58-59)

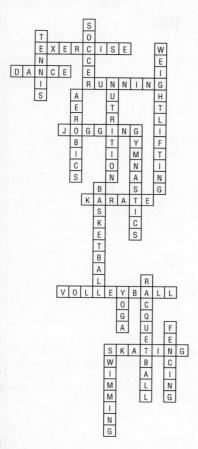

SILLY SOUNDS (page 60)

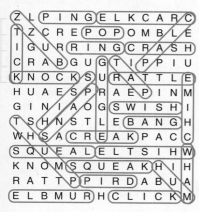

OBSERVE IT (pages 61-62)

1. Leroy
2. Yes
3. No
4. Yes
5. Yes
6. Four
7. Milk, egg, cereal
8. One
9. Yes
10. Yes
11. Pepper
12. Spatula

DOZEN DONUTS (page 62)

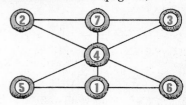

SHOE BUSINESS (page 63)

Woman—high heels	D
Puss—fancy boots	E
Fisherman—waders	F
Ballerina—ballet slippers	E
Diver—flippers	A
Horse—horseshoes	T
Lumberjack—work boots	E
Beach-going girl—open sandals	D

He was not DEFEATED.

SHADOW BOXES (page 64)
Number 3

BRAIN BUSTERS (page 64)
1. Roosters can't lay eggs.
2. He combined them all into one pile.
3. a. Five. Don't forget to count the driver.
   b. Your name. You're the driver.

MAGIC SQUARES (page 65)

C	O	M	E
O	V	A	L
R	E	D	S
K	N	E	E

2	9	4
7	5	3
6	1	8

COUNT ON IT (page 66)
1. The answer will always be the number 2.

MYSTERY GUEST (page 67)
1. MissiSsippi
2. RafT
3. hucklebErrY
4. barefOot
5. MArk TWain

Mystery Guest: TOM SAWYER

YOUR NOSE KNOWS (pages 68-69)

The leftover letters spell:
HOT BUTTERY POPCORN

DELIVERY DAZE (page 74)
You're delivering KUMQUATS.

MYSTERY CROSSWORD (page 75)

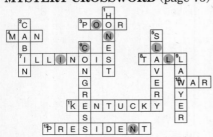

The mystery person is Abraham LINCOLN.

WHAT'S THE FORECAST? (page 80)
1. snow   2. sleet   3. hail   4. wind
5. rain   6. mist   7. thunder
Forecast: WET WEATHER

PRETTY POLLY (page 81)
1. oar	7. pat
2. pot	8. rap
3. rot	9. tap
4. tar	10. art
5. rat	11. roar
6. top	12. port

Bonus puzzle: PORTRAIT

SHADOW BOXES (page 82)
Number 3

BRAIN BUSTERS (page 82)
1. You can see farther at night when you are able to view stars millions of miles away.
2. Fifth letter: E. Tenth letter: J. Twentieth letter: T.
3. We hope you chose the penny option. By the end, you would have received $21,474,836.47.
4. $17. A dozen is twelve so each rose costs a dollar.

INSTRU-MENTAL (page 83)
1. viOlin	6. baSs
2. oRgan	7. Tuba
3. Cymbals	8. peRcussion
4. saxopHones	9. piAno
5. cEllo	

Bonus Word: ORCHESTRA

MOM! (page 84)
1-C, 2-D, 3-B, 4-A

COMMON BONDS (page 85)
1. These objects are filled with air.
2. These objects have stems.
3. These objects have eyes.

LETTER PERFECT (page 86)
1. G   2. O   3. L   4. D
5. S   6. T   7. A   8. R

You get a GOLD STAR.

PICTURE PUZZLES (page 87)
1. square dance	6. jellyfish
2. bread box	7. tomato plant
3. hot dog	8. school of fish
4. palm tree	9. fly ball
5. spelling bee	

SECRET OF THE RINGS (page 88)
THIS WAS THE NAME OF THE FIRST STEAMBOAT ON THE GREAT LAKES.

PRESIDENTS' MONEY MATCH (page 89)
1. B   2. A   3. B   4. C   5. A
6. F   7. G   8. E   9. H   10. D